A Fun, Rhyming, Bible-based Introduction to the Hebrew Alphabet

SARAH MAZOR
YAEL ROSENBERG, Editor
Cover by Benny Rahdiana

Copyright © 2015 Sarah Mazor. All rights reserved.

Published by Lifecodex Publishing, LLC., Mercer Island, Washington.

No part of this publication may be reproduced, stored in a retrieval system, or transmitted in any form or by any means, electronic, mechanical, photocopying, recording, scanning, or otherwise, except as permitted under Section 107 or 108 of the 1976 United States Copyright Act, without the prior written permission of the Publisher.

Requests to the Publisher for permission should be addressed to
Lifecodex Publishing LLC.
PO Box 58, Mercer Island,
WA 98040.
Email: thoughttools@rabbidaniellapin.com

Library of Congress Control Number: 2015955496

ISBN: 0982201842:

AUTHOR'S NOTE

Aleph-Bet: A Fun, Rhyming, Bible-based Introduction to the Hebrew Alphabet is a work of love, or more accurately, a conglomeration of loves: The love of God; the love of His teachings; the love of the Hebrew language; and the love of children.

The ample research that shows that multilingual children fare better at problem solving and are more advanced than their contemporaries in their learning skills, in planning abilities and in self-control, was my initial motivation for writing this book. So what could be better than introducing children to another language, Hebrew, in a fun way while also providing them with an opportunity to connect with the Bible and with Israel?

I hope that you and your children enjoy this book as much as I enjoyed creating it!

Shalom!
Sarah Mazor

In This Book

- The Hebrew Alphabet Chart

- The Sounds of Hebrew Letters

- Guide to Transliteration of Hebrew Words

- The Hebrew Alphabet in Pictures and Rhymes

- The Aleph-Bet Word List: Biblical Sources

- More About Hebrew:

    The Hebrew Alphabet: Interesting Facts

    Hebrew: A Bit of History

The Hebrew Alphabet
The Hebrew Letters are Read from Right to Left

ד dalet	ג gimel	ב vet	בּ bet	א aleph
ט tet	ח chet	ז zayin	ו vav	ה hei
★	ך final chaf	כ chaf	כּ kaf	י yud
	ם final mem	מ mem	ל lamed	★
ע ayin	ס samech	ן final nun	נ nun	
ץ final tzadi	צ tzadi	ף final fei	פ fei	פּ pei
ת tav	שׂ sin	שׁ shin	ר reish	ק kuf

The aleph and the ayin are silent letters. They both take the sound of the vowel that accompanies them. These vowels look like lines and dots that usually appear beneath the letter. The hei too is usually silent when it appears at the end of a word.

The Sounds of the Hebrew Letters

ALEPH is a silent letter*	**LAMED** sounds like the 'l' in lemon
BET sounds like the 'b' in buttons	**MEM** sounds like the 'm' in mommy
VET sounds like the 'v' in vest**	**NUN** sounds like the 'n' in nursery
GIMEL sounds like the 'g' in games	**SAMECH** sounds like the 's' in story
DALET sounds like the 'd' in doll	**AYIN** is a silent letter*
HEI sounds like the 'h' in happy	**PEI** sounds like the 'p' in play
VAV sounds like the 'v' in violet	**FEI** sounds like the 'f' in flower**
ZAYIN sounds like the 'z' in zoo	**TZADI** sounds like the 'tz' in pretzels
CHET sounds like the 'ch' in Bach***	**KUF** sounds like the 'k' in kitten
TET sounds like the 't' in toy	**RESH** sounds like the 'r' in ribbon
YUD sounds like the 'y' in yellow	**SHIN** sounds like the 'sh' in shoes
KAF sounds like the 'k' in kite	**SIN** sounds like the 's' in sky**
CHAF sounds like the 'ch' in Loch Ness**/***	**TAV** sounds like the 't' in television

* Silent letters take on the sound of the vowel that accompanies them
** Alternate sound of same letter (bet/vet, kaf/chaf, pei/fei and shin/sin)
*** The 'CH' sound is like the noise made when clearing one's throat

Guide to Transliteration

a : as in barn
e : as in sled
o : as in go
i : as in me
u : as in glue
ei : as in day
tz : as in pretzel
ch : as in Loch Ness
or the sound you make when clearing your throat

The ALEPH-BET

Tiny little Avi is going to the zoo
To see a big ARYEH and a lioness too

Tiny little Bina loves to drink all day
From her new BAKBUK, its colors red and gray

Tiny little Gadi likes to run and chase
Teeny GESHEM drops and feel 'em on his face

Tiny little Danny wants his pet in his bed
Mom gives him a DUBI to sleep with instead

Tiny little Hadas is no ordinary tyke
When she sees a HAR, she's ready for a hike

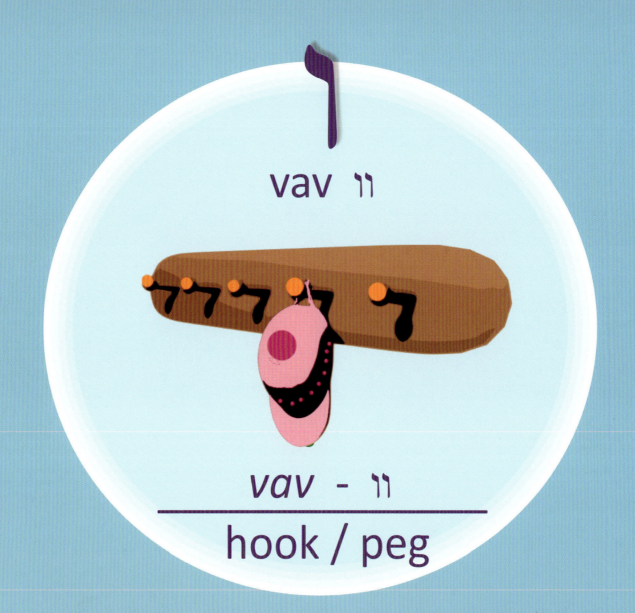

Tiny little Varda hangs the hat she wore
On her very own VAV, right behind the door

Tiny little Zevi is very very cute
He knows that a ZAYIT is actually a fruit

Tiny little Chaim loves to pretend
He is riding a CHAMOR to the home of a friend

Tiny little Tuvia dreams of pots and pans
And being a **TABACH** with lots and lots of fans

Tiny little Yael is incredibly mature
She's a 3-year-old YALDA but people think she's four

Tiny little Kineret asks for a puppy every day
When Mommy buys a KELEV she cheers "hurray!"

Tiny little Leah is helping Mommy bake
Together they're preparing LECHEM and a cake

Tiny little Moshe is now four years old
He gets a MATANA with ribbons red and gold

Tiny little Nili loves her birthday treat
She takes out the NER and then begins to eat

Tiny little Sima loves her daddy's fables
Tales about a SUS who is living in his stables

Tiny little Adina has a real sweet tooth
Yet she shares her UGA with her best friend, Ruth

Tiny little Pnina doesn't like to yell
She rings her PA'AMON, a golden dinner bell

Tiny little Tzipi pretends she is a coach
She blows a TZAFTZEFA as the little kids approach

Tiny little Kobi really wants to know
When it's dark outside, where does KESHET go

reish ריש

rakevet - רכבת

train

Tiny little Rafi loves to travel far
He prefers the RAKEVET to riding in a car

Tiny little Shani wants to befriend
A SHABLUL that she saw around the bend

Tiny little Tami is quite a fine drummer
She banged on the TOF the entire summer

ALEPH – Aryeh / Lion - אַרְיֵה

Will a **lion** roar in the forest, when he has no prey?
--Amos 3:4

הֲיִשְׁאַג אַרְיֵה בַּיַּעַר, וְטֶרֶף אֵין לוֹ.

BET – Bakbuk / Bottle - בַּקְבֻּק

And take in your hand ten loaves and biscuits and a **bottle** of honey and go to him
--I Kings 14:3

וְלָקַחַתְּ בְּיָדֵךְ עֲשָׂרָה לֶחֶם וְנִקֻּדִים, וּבַקְבֻּק דְּבַשׁ וּבָאת אֵלָיו.

GIMEL – Geshem / Rain - גֶּשֶׁם

And it came to pass after a while, that the brook dried up as there was no **rain** in the land.
--I Kings 17:7

וַיְהִי מִקֵּץ יָמִים, וַיִּיבַשׁ הַנָּחַל: כִּי לֹא-הָיָה גֶשֶׁם בָּאָרֶץ.

DALET – Dov / Bear - דֹּב

Better to meet a **bear** robbed of her cubs than a fool in his folly.
--Proverbs 17:12

פָּגוֹשׁ דֹּב שַׁכּוּל בְּאִישׁ; וְאַל כְּסִיל, בְּאִוַּלְתּוֹ.

Note: Dubi is the diminutive for dov.

HEI – Har / Mountain - הַר

And **Mount** Sinai was all smoke because the Lord had descended upon it in fire.
--Exodus 19:18

וְהַר סִינַי, עָשַׁן כֻּלּוֹ, מִפְּנֵי אֲשֶׁר יָרַד עָלָיו ה' בָּאֵשׁ.

VAV – Vav / Hook - וָו

And of the thousand seven hundred seventy five shekels he made **hooks** for the pillars -- Exodus 38:28	וְאֶת־הָאֶלֶף וּשְׁבַע הַמֵּאוֹת וַחֲמִשָּׁה וְשִׁבְעִים עָשָׂה **וָוִים** לָעַמּוּדִים
Note: Vavim - plural for vav	

ZAYIN – Zayit / Olive - זַיִת

And the dove came in to him in the evening and in her mouth a plucked **olive** leaf --Genesis 8:11	וַתָּבֹא אֵלָיו הַיּוֹנָה לְעֵת עֶרֶב, וְהִנֵּה עֲלֵה-**זַיִת** טָרָף בְּפִיהָ

CHET – Chamor / Donkey - חֲמוֹר

If you see your enemy's **donkey** lying under its burden should you refrain from helping him? You must help along with him. --Exodus 23:5	כִּי תִרְאֶה **חֲמוֹר** שֹׂנַאֲךָ רֹבֵץ תַּחַת מַשָּׂאוֹ וְחָדַלְתָּ מֵעֲזֹב לוֹ עָזֹב תַּעֲזֹב עִמּוֹ.

TET – Tabach / Chef - טַבָּח

And the Midianites sold him to Egypt, to Potiphar, Pharaoh's official, the **chief over the food**. --Genesis 37:36	וְהַמְּדָנִים מָכְרוּ אֹתוֹ אֶל מִצְרָיִם לְפוֹטִיפַר סְרִיס פַּרְעֹה שַׂר **הַטַּבָּחִים**.
Note: Tabachim - plural for tabach	

YUD – Yeled / Child - יֶלֶד

And Michal the daughter of Saul had no **child** until her death.
--II Samuel 6:23

וּלְמִיכַל, בַּת-שָׁאוּל, לֹא-הָיָה לָהּ, **יֶלֶד** עַד, יוֹם מוֹתָהּ.

Note: Yeled is male child, yalda is female child

KAF – Kelev / Dog - כֶּלֶב

But against all the children of Israel not a **dog** whet his tongue
--Exodus 11:7

וּלְכֹל בְּנֵי יִשְׂרָאֵל, לֹא יֶחֱרַץ **כֶּלֶב** לְשֹׁנוֹ

LAMED – Lechem / Bread - לֶחֶם

By the sweat of your brow you shall eat **bread**
--Genesis 3:19

בְּזֵעַת אַפֶּיךָ תֹּאכַל **לֶחֶם**

MEM – Matana / Gift / Present - מַתָּנָה

Oppression turns a wise man foolish; and a **gift** destroys the heart.
--Ecclesiastes 7:7

כִּי הָעֹשֶׁק, יְהוֹלֵל חָכָם; וִיאַבֵּד אֶת-לֵב, **מַתָּנָה**.

NUN – Ner / Candle - נֵר

A commandment is a **candle**, and the Torah is light
--Proverbs 6:23

כִּי **נֵר** מִצְוָה וְתוֹרָה אוֹר

SAMECH – Sus / Horse - סוּס

A **horse** is prepared for a day of battle, but the victory belongs to God.
--Proverbs 21:31

סוּס מוּכָן לְיוֹם מִלְחָמָה וְלַה' הַתְּשׁוּעָה.

AYIN – Uga / Cake - עֻגָה

A Elijah said to her, *Do not fear. Come and do as you say. But first make for me from there a small* **cake**
--I Kings 17:13

וַיֹּאמֶר אֵלֶיהָ אֵלִיָּהוּ אַל תִּירְאִי בֹּאִי עֲשִׂי כִדְבָרֵךְ אַךְ עֲשִׂי לִי מִשָּׁם **עֻגָה** קְטַנָּה בָרִאשֹׁנָה

PEI – Pa'amon / Bell - פַּעֲמֹן

A golden **bell** and a pomegranate, a golden **bell** and a pomegranate, all around on the hem of the robe.
--Exodus 28:34

פַּעֲמֹן זָהָב וְרִמּוֹן **פַּעֲמֹן** זָהָב וְרִמּוֹן עַל שׁוּלֵי הַמְּעִיל סָבִיב.

TZADI – Tzaftzefa / Whistle - צַפְצֵפָה

And brought low you shall speak from the ground, and your speech shall be low from the dust; and your voice shall be ghostlike from the ground, and your speech shall **chirp** out of the dust.
--Isaiah 29:4

וְשָׁפַלְתְּ מֵאֶרֶץ תְּדַבֵּרִי, וּמֵעָפָר תִּשַּׁח אִמְרָתֵךְ; וְהָיָה כְּאוֹב מֵאֶרֶץ, קוֹלֵךְ, וּמֵעָפָר, אִמְרָתֵךְ **תְּצַפְצֵף**.

Note: The root letters for 'tzaftzefa', a whistle that makes a sharp noise, is the same root in the word 'tetzaftzef' – to chirp or to produce high piercing noise.

KUF – Keshet / Rainbow - קֶשֶׁת

And when I cause clouds to come upon the earth, and then the **rainbow** will appear in the cloud.
--Genesis 9:14

וְהָיָה בְּעַנְנִי עָנָן עַל הָאָרֶץ וְנִרְאֲתָה הַ**קֶּשֶׁת** בֶּעָנָן.

REISH – Rakevet / Train - רַכֶּבֶת

Some put their faith in **chariots**, some in horses, but we mention the name of the Lord our God.
--Psalms 20:8

אֵלֶּה בָ**רֶכֶב**, וְאֵלֶּה בַסּוּסִים וַאֲנַחְנוּ, בְּשֵׁם ה' אֱלֹהֵינוּ נַזְכִּיר.

Note: Trains did not exist in Biblical times however, the modern mode of transportation, the 'rakevet', has Biblical origins. The root letters for 'rakevet' is Reish/Chaf/Vet, same as the root for 'rechev', the Chariot mentioned in the passage above. The letters Reish/Chaf/Vet are also the root of 'rochev', rider (n.), riding (v.).

SHIN – Shablul / Snail - שַׁבְּלוּל

Like a **snail**, which melts and passes away, like a stillbirth of a mole that never sees the sun.
--Psalms 58:9

כְּמוֹ **שַׁבְּלוּל** תֶּמֶס יַהֲלֹךְ נֵפֶל אֵשֶׁת בַּל חָזוּ שָׁמֶשׁ.

TAV – Tof / Drum - תֹּף

And Miriam the prophetess, the sister of Aaron, took the **timbrel** in her hand and all the women went out after her with timbrels and with dances.
--Exodus 15:20

וַתִּקַּח מִרְיָם הַנְּבִיאָה אֲחוֹת אַהֲרֹן, אֶת-הַ**תֹּף** בְּיָדָהּ; וַתֵּצֶאןָ כָל-הַנָּשִׁים אַחֲרֶיהָ, בְּתֻפִּים וּבִמְחֹלֹת.

Note: A timbrel is a percussion instrument, a type of drum.

The Hebrew Alphabet: Interesting Facts

Hebrew is different than English not only in sound but also in the way it is written. The Hebrew alphabet has 22 letters. Five of the 22 letters are written a bit differently when they appear at the end of a word. They are the Kaf Sofit, Mem Sofit, Nun Sofit, Pei Sofit, and Tzadi sofit, (Sofit means final).

Some Hebrew letters have more than one sound. For example, the sound of 'P' and the sound of 'F' are represented by the same letter, pronounced 'Pei' or 'Fei'

Hebrew vowels are represented by symbols. The vowels are generally not written in texts though they are used in prayer books and beginner Hebrew reading and learning books.

The most observable distinction between Hebrew and the western languages is that Hebrew is written and read from right to left.

Hebrew: A Bit of History

The Hebrew language, the language of the Bible, was spoken by Jews in the Land of Israel in ancient times. It has been in constant use as the language of prayer during thousands of years in exile. The language was revived as a spoken language in the 1800s by Eliezer Ben-Yehuda, the father of Modern Hebrew. Hebrew is the official language of the State of Israel.

Modern Hebrew accommodates modern-day's societal, environmental and cultural evolutions as well as new scientific understanding, technological development and new-age innovation. Though Hebrew words are available for modern-day phenomena, English, Latin and other international words infiltrated the contemporary Hebrew-speaking individual's vocabulary, with words such as telephone, televizia (television), bacteria, or autobus, to name a few. However, Hebrew language purists and lovers of the ancient yet living language are cognizant of the fact that Hebrew words exist for modern innovation and that they are often based on the roots of words that are found in the Bible.

For example, the Hebrew word for 'train' is RAKEVET and for 'vehicle' is RECHEV. Both share the root of Reish/Kaf/Vet, which is also the root of ROCHEV, a rider (n.) or the act of riding (v.).

Another example: Computer is MACHSHEV. Its root of Chet/Shin/Vet is the same for CHOSHEV, a thinker (n.) or thinks (v.). LACHSHOV is to think and MACHSHEVON is a calculator. (See Esther 8:3 אשר חשב על היהודים - that [Haman] **thought** to do to the Jews.).

You can see that the root words Reish/Kaf/Vet (רכב) and Chet/Shin/Vet (חשב) are Biblical in origin even though there were no trains or computers in ancient times. (Note: Bet/Vet = same letter / Kaf/Chaf = same letter)